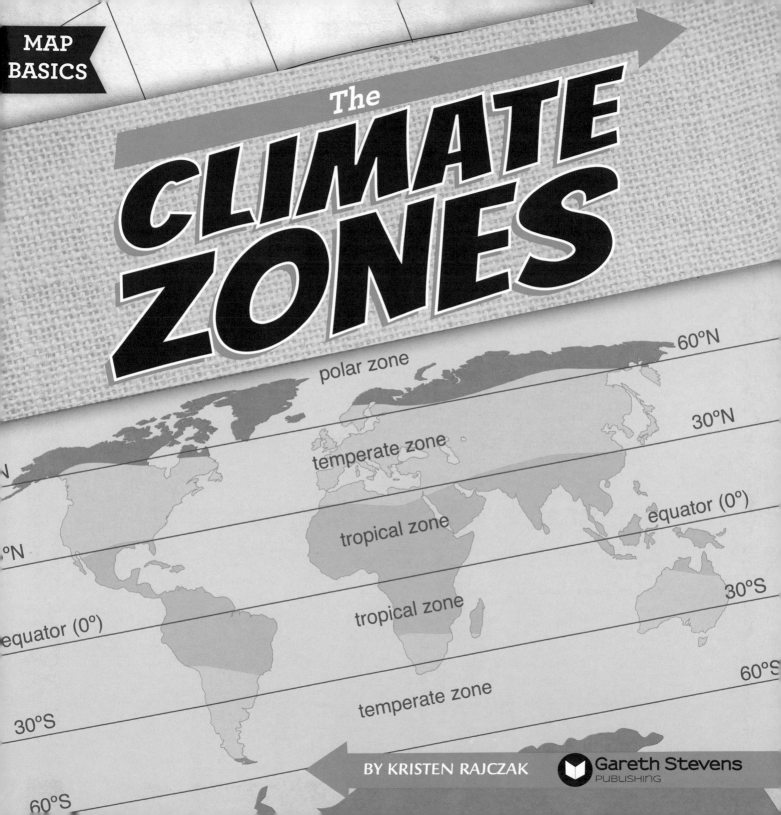

MAP
BASICS

The

CLIMATE ZONES

polar zone

60°N

temperate zone

30°N

tropical zone

equator (0°)

N

tropical zone

30°S

equator (0°)

temperate zone

60°S

30°S

BY KRISTEN RAJCZAK

Gareth Stevens
PUBLISHING

60°S

Please visit our website, www.garethstevens.com. For a free color catalog of all our high-quality books, call toll free 1-800-542-2595 or fax 1-877-542-2596.

Library of Congress Cataloging-in-Publication Data

Rajczak, Kristen.
Climate zones / by Kristen Rajczak.
  p. cm. — (Map basics)
Includes index.
ISBN 978-1-4824-0801-0 (pbk.)
ISBN 978-1-4824-1088-4 (6-pack)
ISBN 978-1-4824-0800-3 (library binding)
1. Map reading — Juvenile literature. 2. Climatology — Juvenile literature. I. Rajczak, Kristen. II. Title.
GA130.R35 2015
551.6022—d23

First Edition

Published in 2015 by
Gareth Stevens Publishing
111 East 14th Street, Suite 349
New York, NY 10003

Designer: Sarah Liddell
Editor: Kristen Rajczak

Photo credits: Cover, pp. 1, 7, 13 Agrus/Shutterstock.com; p. 5 dem10/E+/Getty Images; p. 9 (main) David McNew/Getty Images News/Getty Images; p. 9 (steppe) Pichugin Dmitry/ Shutterstock.com; p. 11 Mark Kolbe/Getty Images News/Getty Images; p. 15 Julie Harris/E+/Getty Images; p. 17 David Sucsy/E+/Getty Images; p. 19 George Rose/Getty Images News/Getty Images.

Printed in the United States of America

CPSIA compliance information: Batch #CS15GS: For further information contact Gareth Stevens, New York, New York at 1-800-542-2595.

CONTENTS

Words in the glossary appear in **bold** type the first time they are used in the text.

WHAT'S THE CLIMATE?

Do you live somewhere that has four seasons, like Vermont or New York? Maybe you've visited southern Italy, where it's warm and sunny much of the year. If you go north to Norway, expect winter nights to be especially cold, dark, and long.

The average weather conditions of a place, or climate, include how much **precipitation** an area gets each year and its range of **temperatures**. These are affected by **latitude**, winds, and nearness to mountains or a body of water.

JUST THE FACTS

A climatologist (kly-muh-TAH-luh-jihst) is a scientist who studies climate, climate changes, and how climate affects an area.

Depending on the time of day and time of year, parts of Earth may be facing toward or away from the sun. The amount of sunlight a place gets affects its climate.

Earth can be divided into climate zones, or areas. One way to separate the globe into zones is by latitude ranges and the air masses in each. Low-latitude climates are affected by **tropical** air, while high-latitude climates are controlled by Arctic air masses. These two kinds of air masses meet in the midlatitudes.

More often, Earth is divided into six climate zones based on the shared features of areas' climates. This book will cover the following climate zones:

- dry, or arid
- highland
- Mediterranean
- tropical
- temperate
- polar

JUST THE FACTS

These six climate zones are similar to the general groupings in the Köppen-Geiger-Pohl climate **classification** system. This system uses capital letters A, B, C, D, E, and H to stand for the different climate zones.

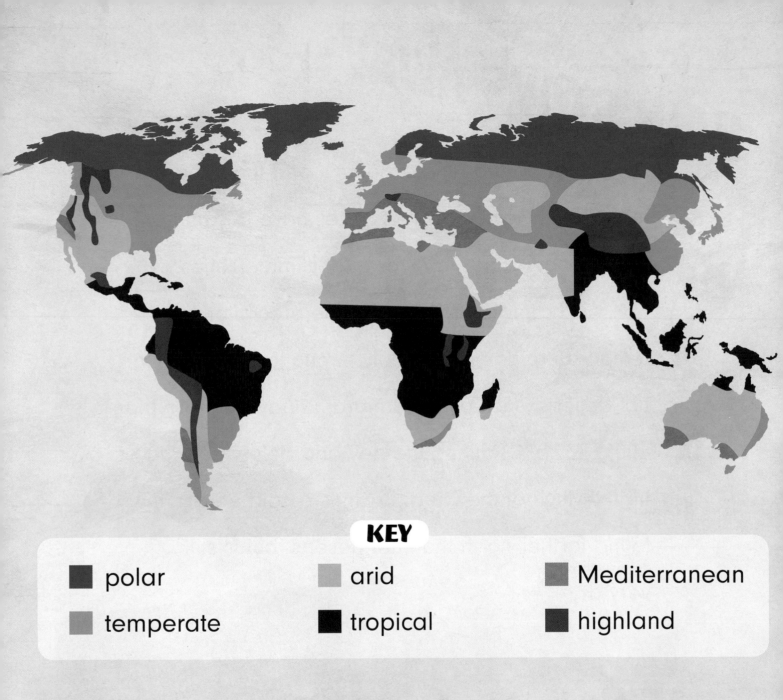

KEY

- ■ polar
- ■ temperate
- ■ arid
- ■ tropical
- ■ Mediterranean
- ■ highland

The map key shows which color on the map represents which climate zone.

RAIN STAYS AWAY

What do the African Sahara and the Great Basin in the southwestern United States have in common? They're both part of dry, or arid, climate zones.

Arid climate zones have little precipitation. The temperature can vary widely throughout the day. In hot deserts, such as the Sahara, it may be more than 100°F (37.8°C) during the day and below freezing at night! Much of the Great Basin is a cold desert. It's found farther north than hot deserts, but is still very dry.

JUST THE FACTS
Steppes are part of arid climate zones. These large areas have no trees and don't get much rain. There are steppes in southeast Europe and Asia.

steppe in Mongolia

Arid climates such as that of Death Valley, shown here, take up about 25 percent of Earth's land surface.

Look back at the map on page 7. Each climate zone is just one color that matches the map key. But by traveling around the world, you would find that climate zones overlap and can be divided into even smaller zones.

Tropical climate zones, which are close to the **equator**, are hot! Some parts are hot and arid, while others, like the Amazon rainforest, are hot and **humid**. In the tropical climate zones of southern Africa and India, there's a wet season and dry season.

JUST THE FACTS

Nearness to the equator is one of the biggest factors determining the climate of an area. The closer an area is, the hotter it is and the more often the sun shines!

Many climatologists say plant life is the best way to see climate in action. Many green plants, such as in this rainforest, show an area that gets plenty of sun and rain for them to grow well.

11

Mediterranean climate zones aren't just near the Mediterranean Sea, though that's the area the zone is named for. Mediterranean climates can be found mainly near water between 30° and 45° north latitude, 30° and 45° south latitude, and on the western sides of **continents**.

This climate zone has hot, dry summers, and mild winters. However, the climate changes a bit depending on how close an area is to water. Inland, the summers are hotter and the winters are cooler.

JUST THE FACTS

The Mediterranean climate zone is also called "dry summer subtropical" climate.

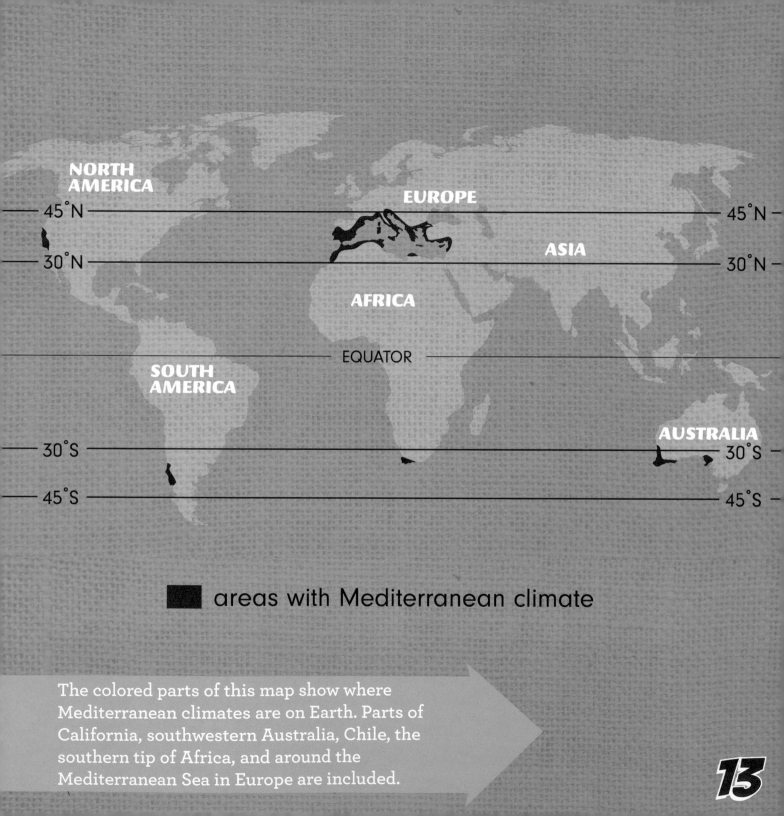

NORTH
AMERICA

EUROPE

ASIA

45°N

30°N

AFRICA

EQUATOR

SOUTH
AMERICA

AUSTRALIA

30°S

45°S

areas with Mediterranean climate

The colored parts of this map show where
Mediterranean climates are on Earth. Parts of
California, southwestern Australia, Chile, the
southern tip of Africa, and around the
Mediterranean Sea in Europe are included.

13

The polar climate zone includes both the North and the South Poles. Greenland and the northernmost parts of North America also have a polar climate, as do northern Europe and Russia.

These zones are cold and dry. Temperatures often only rise above freezing about 4 months out of the year. Only the top layer of soil thaws in polar climates, so plants and trees are small and few. The lowest temperature ever recorded was at the Vostok II Research Station in Antarctica. It was –129°F (–89.4°C)!

JUST THE FACTS
Antarctica is so dry, it can be classified as a desert.

Polar regions have plenty of snow and ice, especially at the higher latitudes.

Temperate climate zones have cold winters and mild summers. These are areas that have four seasons—spring, summer, fall, and winter.

If you live somewhere the leaves change color in the fall, then you live in a temperate climate zone. In fact, temperate climate zones often have many trees. Some grasslands, such as the Great Plains in the United States, have few trees, but still have a temperate climate. Asia, South America, and Africa all have temperate grasslands, too.

JUST THE FACTS

Temperate climate zones are sometimes called "continental" climate zones. That's because they're generally in the middle of continents.

Cherry blossoms are a sure sign of spring in temperate Washington, DC, where many cherry trees grow.

Highland or mountain climate zones can be found in the Andes of South America, the Himalayas of Asia, and the Eastern Highlands of Africa. This zone isn't always included in classification systems because highland areas are found within other climate zones. Also, as the **altitudes** and natural features of these areas are different, it's hard to list qualities that apply to the climate of all mountainous areas.

In general, highland climate zones have cooler temperatures and more precipitation than the nearby lowland climate zone.

JUST THE FACTS

As altitude of a highland area increases, temperature decreases.

In North America, the Rocky Mountains, Cascades, and Sierra Nevada would all be grouped in the highland climate zone. Check out the snow on the peaks of the Canadian Rockies, shown here!

THE CLIMES ARE CHANGING

Our planet's climate was once very different than it is today. Climate change has occurred many times in Earth's history. The climate change we face today isn't part of this natural cycle. It's caused by people's actions. Pollution and the burning of fossil fuels are causing Earth to warm up!

You can help slow climate change. Turn your electronics off when you aren't using them. Walk or ride your bike as much as possible. Don't litter! Together, we can save our climate zones.

JUST THE FACTS

Fossil fuels are the coal, oil, and natural gas that form deep within Earth from plant and animal remains.

CLIMATE ZONE BASICS

ZONE	FEATURES
arid	dry; temperature can vary greatly
highland	cooler temperatures and more precipitation than the climate zone around it
Mediterranean	hot, dry summers and mild winters; cooler temperatures farther inland
polar	cold; dry
temperate	four seasons with warm summers and cold winters
tropical	hot; can be humid or dry

GLOSSARY

altitude: height above sea level

classification: grouping

continent: one of Earth's seven great landmasses. They are North America, South America, Antarctica, Asia, Africa, Australia, and Europe.

equator: an imaginary line around Earth that is the same distance from the North and the South Poles

humid: containing moisture

latitude: the imaginary lines that run east and west above and below the equator

precipitation: rain, snow, sleet, or hail

temperature: how hot or cold something is

tropical: having to do with the warm parts of Earth near the equator

FOR MORE INFORMATION

BOOKS

Baker, Stuart. *In Temperate Zones*. New York, NY: Marshall Cavendish Benchmark, 2010.

Birch, Robin. *Earth's Climate*. New York, NY: Marshall Cavendish Benchmark, 2009.

WEBSITES

Artic Animal Pictures
kids.nationalgeographic.com/kids/photos/arctic-animals/
Check out photographs of animals that live in the polar climate zone.

Geography4Kids.com: Climate
www.geography4kids.com/files/climate_intro.html
Learn about the different climates around the world as well as other awesome earth science information.

INDEX